BRITAIN IN OLD PH

CHISLEHURST
& SIDCUP

JOHN MERCER

SUTTON PUBLISHING LIMITED

Sutton Publishing Limited
Phoenix Mill · Thrupp · Stroud
Gloucestershire · GL5 2BU

First published 1998

Title page: Look-out tower on Chislehurst
Common, 1914–18.

British Library Cataloguing in Publication Data
A catalogue record for this book is available from the
British Library.

ISBN 0-7509-1551-X

Typeset in 10/12 Perpetua.
Typesetting and origination by
Sutton Publishing Limited.
Printed in Great Britain by
Ebenezer Baylis, Worcester.

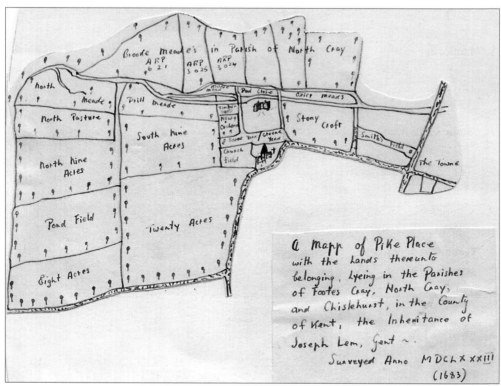

Copy of an old map showing the position of the former manor house of Foots Cray behind All Saints'
church. This manor house was demolished when Foots Cray Place was built in the eighteenth century.
Archaeologists have found the footings.

CONTENTS

Chislehurst village sign depicting Queen Elizabeth I knighting Thomas Walsingham of Scadbury in 1597 for services rendered. The sign was erected in 1953 to commemorate the coronation of Queen Elizabeth II.

INTRODUCTION

The area covered by this set of photographs is that of the former Chislehurst and Sidcup Urban District. It covered an area of 8,597 acres and was formed in 1934 combining a number of neighbourhood units, which though administered by one authority retained many of their local characteristics. Chislehurst and Sidcup were the chief centres of the district with Mottingham in the north-west corner, and St Paul's Cray, Foots Cray and North Cray in the east. The authority was broken up in 1965 when Chislehurst, Mottingham and St Paul's Cray went into the newly formed London Borough of Bromley and Sidcup, and Foots Cray and North Cray were absorbed into the London Borough of Bexley.

In the early nineteenth century Sidcup was a small village lying largely in the parish of Chislehurst and partly in that of Foots Cray. The boundary between the two parishes ran along what is now Sidcup High Street and the narrow tree-lined Rectory Lane which was a section of the old road between London and Maidstone. When the New Cross Turnpike Trust improved the road in 1781, Sidcup Hill was opened up through the parish of Chislehurst. A mark on the south side of the brick bridge over the River Cray in Foots Cray village indicates that this was a boundary mark for Chislehurst parish. Early in the twentieth century North Cray, Lamorbey, Halfway Street and Blackfen were added to Sidcup – the last three areas having previously been part of the parish of Bexley.

The area's oldest buildings are the Domesday churches of Foots Cray, North Cray and St Paul's Cray, though all have been rebuilt within the last 150 years. These were the sites of the earliest settlements along the River Cray. Chislehurst though an early settlement did not get St Nicholas' church until a century after the Norman Conquest.

Chislehurst and to a lesser extent Sidcup became the home of the nobility and of wealthy London merchants in centuries past. The endemic plague drove the rich out of London during the sixteenth and seventeenth centuries. Scadbury became the home of the Walsinghams; the historian William Camden lived in a house at the site of the present Camden Place, the Sydneys occupied Frognal; Lord Bexley acquired Foots Cray Place; and Lord Castlereagh relaxed from his duties as Foreign Secretary in what has become Loring Hall. The French Imperial Family in exile added lustre to Chislehurst, and the Berens, the Malcolms and the Lewins brought money and taste to Sidcup and Lamorbey.

Although Chislehurst has always been regarded as socially superior to Sidcup, it is noteworthy that Sidcup has retained the footprints of the former large estates in Foots Cray Meadows, Lamorbey Park, The Hollies and Sidcup Place. Nevertheless because of its scattered nature and its careful preservation of the Common, Chislehurst presents much attractive and unspoiled land.

Both Chislehurst and Sidcup were opened up to commuter development by the coming of the railway but the vast infilling of rows and rows of houses on previous farmland or woodland did not occur until the 1920s and '30s. Many fine Victorian and Edwardian houses survived the development but most of these are to be found in Chislehurst. The greater part of built-up suburbia is to be found in Sidcup.

The frenetic A20 is now the dividing line between Chislehurst and Sidcup. But it must be remembered that a considerable slice of what is now Sidcup was once known as East Chislehurst and the tie between the two areas was once much stronger than it is now. The separation of the two in 1965 was bitterly opposed by many in Sidcup because they considered the relationship to Chislehurst, and therefore Bromley, to be much closer than that to Bexley. Time has healed the wounds.

WAR OFFICE   25th November 1914

His Majesty The King has been graciously pleased to approve of the grant of the Victoria Cross to the undermentioned Officers, Non-Commissioned Officers and Men, for conspicuous bravery whilst serving with the Expeditionary Force:—

Rank	13814 Private
Name	Sidney Frank Godley
Corps, etc.	4th Battalion Royal Fusiliers City of London Regiment
Action for which commended	For coolness and gallantry in fighting his machine gun under a hot fire for two hours after he had been wounded at Mons on 23 August
LONDON GAZETTE	November 1914 Page 9957 LONDON GAZETTE.

Notification of the award of the Victoria Cross to Frank Godley in 1914. He was a Sidcup lad who held a bridge over the Mons Canal at Nimy in August 1914. He is remembered in the name given to sheltered accommodation in Etfield Way, Sidcup.

CHAPTER ONE

STATELY HOMES

Chislehurst and Sidcup had many stately homes. Some have survived but are no longer the houses of great families and have now been put to other uses. Lamorbey Park has become Rose Bruford College of Speech and Drama. Farringtons has been rebuilt as a school. Sidcup Place is being developed as a restaurant. Others were less lucky. Foots Cray Place was destroyed by fire; North Cray Place was pulled down to make way for housing. The Hollies house is falling down. Holbrook is barely a memory. The illustrations that follow chart the history of many a fine house – a decline from gracious living but not necessarily a fall from grace.

Frognal in the seventeenth century. Its origins go back at least to the eleventh century. Structurally the house was a hollow square with a detached outbuilding. The grounds were laid out formally with a straight tree-lined avenue, fruit plantations, a sheltered winter garden and a kitchen garden. It was the major house in what was known as East Chislehurst.

Frognal from the east, *c.* 1950.

The former entrance to Frognal from Watery Lane. On the left is the coach house. This was demolished in the late 1960s when the new Queen Mary's Hospital was planned.

Frognal house and grounds became a hospital dedicated to plastic surgery during the First World War. Major Geddes was the pioneering surgeon. There is a ward named after him in the new general hospital on the site. The original hospital was hutted and the huts can be seen at the top of this picture taken in about 1940.

The military hospital became a general hospital in 1930. This photograph shows a sister and a staff nurse in the grounds during a fund-raising fete. The small boy on the left is the author's son who was in the hospital at the time (c. 1962). The new hospital was opened by Barbara Castle, the Secretary of State for Health in 1974. The first part to be built was the maternity wing; this covered the old ice house belonging to Frognal. Before the coming of refrigeration meat and game would be stored underground with ice collected during the winter months.

Farrington's School in Perry Street. This was opened in 1911 as a girls' school under the aegis of the Methodist Church. The site had been occupied by a graceful Jacobean house owned by General Thomas Farrington who raised a regiment and fought under Marlborough at Ramilles in 1706.

Chesil House in St Paul's Road dates from the 1770s. Nikolaus Pevsner in *Buildings of England* (1969) described it as the best eighteenth-century house in Chislehurst.

Hawkwood was situated at the end of Hawkwood Lane. It was built in a conglomeration of styles on a site once known as Mann's Farm. Its most celebrated occupants were the Edlmann family. Colonel Edlmann was a founder of the British Legion and a benefactor to Chislehurst, purchasing part of Petts Wood to prevent it falling into the hands of speculative builders.

The drawing room at Hawkwood in its Edwardian heyday.

An old print of Foots Cray Place built by Bourchier Cleve, a London merchant, in about 1765 in Palladian style. The house passed to the Harenc family and then to Lord Bexley who lived there from 1821 until his death in 1851. As Nicholas Vansittart, he was Chancellor of the Exchequer for eleven years and introduced the word 'budget' into the Treasury.

Foots Cray Place at the turn of the twentieth century. Lord Waring (of Waring and Gillows) made it his home. He was a great Scouter and had jamborees in the park.

The farm entrance to Foots Cray Place around 1900. The paling fence has gone but the farm cottage is still there having been modernized.

The pavilion built for games by Lord Waring, 1970s. By the time this picture was taken it had been allowed to deteriorate. It has since been bought from Bexley Borough and is now an elegant private house. Foots Cray Meadows are open to the public and support many species of flora.

Foxbury in Kemnal Lane, 1950s. It stands on the site of an ancient manor house and was built for the wealthy Tiarks family in the 1870s. It became a missionary college and is now a training centre for a building society.

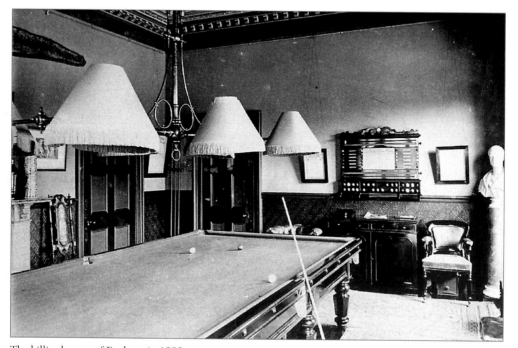

The billiard room of Foxbury in 1983.

The Manor House on the Green, Sidcup, 1960. It was built in 1790 and was originally called Place Green House. Never a real manor house, as there never was a Sidcup manor, it became a girls' school and today it has been well renovated as the Register Office.

The Hollies, Lamorbey. This was built for the Lewin family in about 1845. There had been an earlier Tudor house called Marrowbone Hall. The Hollies became the administrative centre for the Children's Home built by the Board of Guardians for Deptford and Greenwich in 1900. It is now falling into decay.

North Cray Place in 1818, the seat of H. Meux, the brewer. It was demolished after bomb damage in the Second World War and new housing was built on the site.

Holbrook, a seventeenth-century house once at the bottom of Holbrook Lane, Chislehurst. Poyntell Crescent, named after former owners, covers some of the old site.

Sidcup House, also confusingly known as Sidcup Place, was a Queen Anne house. This photograph shows the property shortly before it was demolished in 1929. St John's Road is seen behind the petrol pumps.

Demolition of Sidcup House in 1929. Dame Ethel Smythe, the composer, lived there as a child. Her father was garrison commander at Woolwich in the 1850s.

Lamorbey House at the turn of the twentieth century. The first house at Lamorbey was Tudor. The one seen today was built by William Steele, a director of the East India Company, in 1748. It was considerably added to by the Malcolm family in 1842, following a Jacobean style designed by John Shaw.

The lake at Lamorbey House.

This view shows the east side of Lamorbey House with the library.

In 1910 Lamorbey Park became a hotel run by a Mr Shepherd. A frequent visitor was the novelist Ursula Bloom who wrote several books under the influence of its then rural charm. After the Second World War it became an Adult Education Centre: this photograph was taken during the early 1950s when it was still used for that purpose. Today it is the Rose Bruford College of Speech and Drama. The orangery and music room look out over the lawns. The music room, which was badly damaged by fire a few years ago, has been carefully restored.

The former Chislehurst rectory in Church Lane, c. 1895. It was demolished in 1960 because it was too large for contemporary clergy use. Before the coming of the motor car a clergy house had to be large enough to accommodate a visiting bishop and his servants as well as the rector's own family and servants.

Demolition of the rectory in progress. A pity it could not have converted into flats rather than being destroyed.

An illustration of North Cray Cottage, later known as Wollett Hall, by Virtue, 1820. This was the country home of Lord Castlereagh, Foreign Secretary at the time of Waterloo and after. He committed suicide in his bedroom in 1822.

This is the same property from North Clay Road aspect and today it is a nursing home known as Loring Hall.

Scadbury, home of the Walsinghams, *c.* 1900. Sir Thomas Walsingham was knighted by Queen Elizabeth in 1599. His cousin, Sir Francis, was Secretary of State to the same queen. The Walsinghams' estate was bought by Sir Richard Bettenson whose descendant, Thomas Townshend, pulled down the medieval moated house in 1730 and moved the family to Frognal. Only some walls and the moat are to be found today and the estate is now a public park and wildlife sanctuary.

Sidcup Place when a school, 1920. It was built in 1743 and added to extensively by the Berens family in the nineteenth century. In 1934 it became the council offices for the newly formed Chislehurst and Sidcup Urban District Council.

The stables and tower built by the Berens. It has now been sold to Whitbread's to create a restaurant, but it is a Grade II listed building and the exterior must be preserved.

St Paul's Cray Hill, off Chapmans Lane, after the Second World War. Nothing remains of this fine Tudor building, which was demolished in the 1950s, but it has given its name to a park.

St Paul's Cray Common joins on to Petts Wood. It was a favourite walk of the exiled French Emperor Napoleon III while he still had his health.

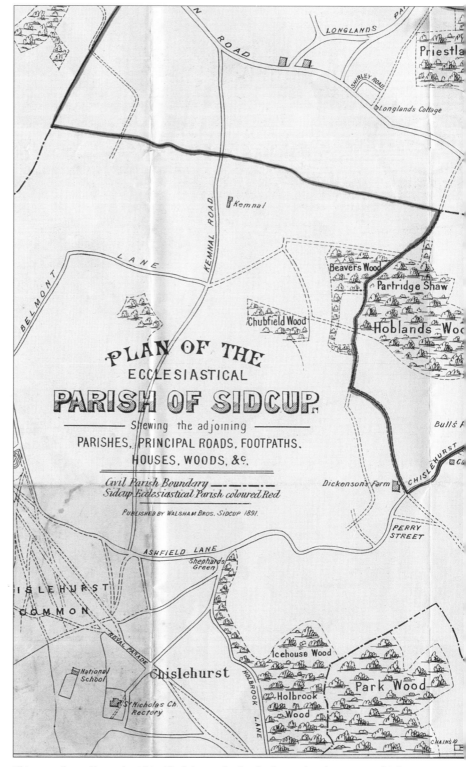

This map shows Frognal within Chislehurst. It clearly shows also the extent of Sidcup

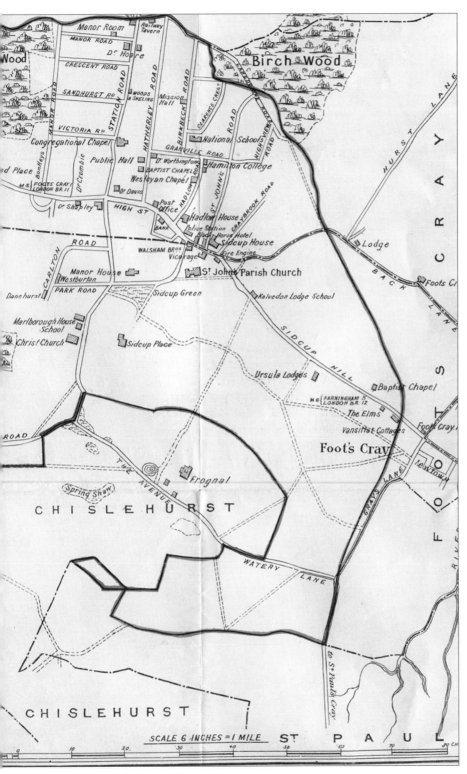

within the parish of St John's, *c.* 1890.

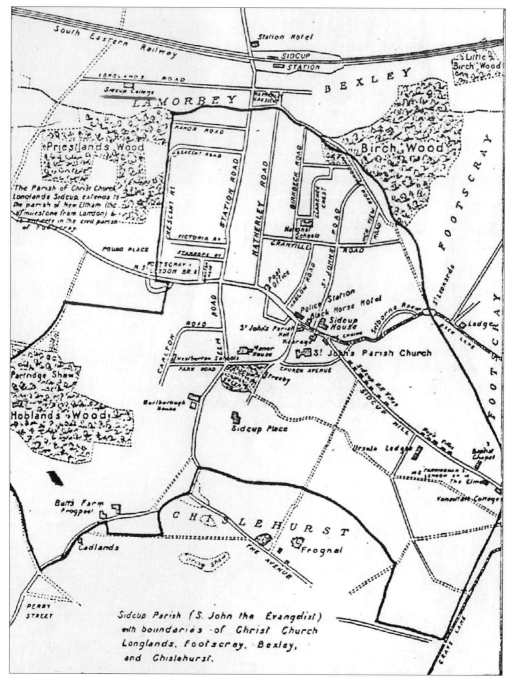

This ecclesiastical map of 1888 shows Lamorbey as part of Bexley. Notice the amount of woodland: Birchwood, Priestlands Wood and Hoblands Wood.

CHAPTER TWO

CHISLEHURST

The name of Chislehurst comes from the Saxon 'ceosol' meaning gravel and 'hyrst' meaning wood. Scadbury was probably the first settlement in the area and was originally a hunting lodge. Cottages grew up around the Scadbury estate, making Perry Street and Scadbury Lane the nucleus of the early village. There were no houses on the site of the present village or in Church Road until the early 1800s. The plague drove people out of London to live in Chislehurst and among those who came in the seventeenth century were historian William Camden and wealthy merchants like the Poyntells, the Cunliffes and the Blencarnes.

The present village, originally known as Prickend, developed in the second half of the nineteenth century. Once the Commons were preserved by Act of Parliament in 1886, the clusters of houses and shops that make Chislehurst were firmly located and with the coming of the railway in 1865, the population began to grow quickly. In 1801, 1,217 people lived there; by 1851, 2,088; by 1881, 3,814; and by 1891, 5,069. Except at the Mottingham end, Chislehurst has been spared the fate of becoming an urban sprawl and today includes many fine modern houses which give the district a deceptively rural appearance.

The Lodge and gates in Kemnal Road leading to Foxbury at the beginning of the twentieth century.

The crossroads by the cricket ground, *c.* 1914. The entrance to Camden Place is on the left behind the trees. The Cedars, home of William Willet the inventor of the idea of British Summer Time, is behind the cart.

Prickend Pond, *c.* 1914. This was once a gravel pit.

The thatched cottage in Perry Street. On the back of the postcard, dated 1913, is written to a Miss Anderson of Shepherds Bush: 'Dear Polly, just a line thanks V. much for PC. I am on duty 1st Sunday in April so shall not be able to see you only when I am off duty, Your living sister Ciss'. The writer must have been in service.

Perry Street between the two world wars. It took its name from the pear orchards through which it passed.

Ambulances in Chislehurst in 1915. It would seem that they were waiting in convoy to go to France.

Another view of Prickend Pond from Heathfield Lane, *c.* 1900.

The windmill on the eastern edge of the cricket field, 1876. It was built in 1796.

The demolition of the parish windmill in 1876 by a Mr Baskcomb. He incurred the wrath of the parishioners who pulled down his fences each time he tried to enclose the land for development. The land was retained for the commons in the end.

The Queen's Head by Prickend Pond at the top of the High Street, *c.* 1900.

The Bull's Head at the corner of Church Road and St Paul's Cray Road, *c.* 1900. Notice the narrow wheel tracks.

The High Street on the coronation day of King George V and Queen Mary in 1911.

Queuing for a bus on Whit Monday in the High Street, *c.* 1920.

Chislehurst High Street. Only two carts are in sight, *c.* 1910.

Again the High Street but this time there is one car, *c.* 1929.

A bonfire party on the Green near the Cockpit. Is this for the 1911 coronation? The crowds seem too lightly dressed for a 5 November bonfire.

St Nicholas' church, coronation day, 1911. The spectators are watching a tableau.

Bickley Hotel, Old Hill in 1913. Note the horse-drawn charabanc.

Old Hill, *c.* 1913. This was the main road to Bromley before Summer Hill was opened to the public in 1865.

Chislehurst Caves, 1920s. Originally these were chalk and flint mines. The earliest recorded reference to them is in a charter written in 1250. They became an Edwardian tourist attraction. They were used to store ammunition during the First World War and as a huge air raid shelter in the Second World War. As many as 2,000 people used them every night during the V1 and V2 attacks of 1944 and 1945.

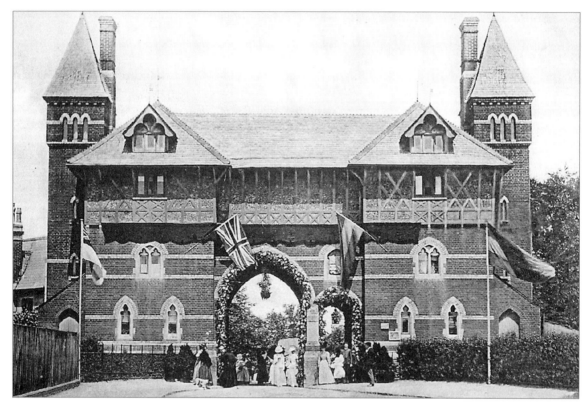

The Water Tower at the top of Summer Hill. It was built as a gatehouse to Mr Wythes' estate in 1860 but was pulled down in 1963 as a hazard to motorists. The author recalls as a boy riding through the narrow gateway on his bicycle and zooming down the steep hill on the other side.

Martin's Bank and Summerhill Vale, *c.* 1900. The Water Tower is on the left.

Mill Place and Susan Wood are set in a dip and at one time were almost one self-contained community. There was a school and a church. Both buildings were later put to commercial use but now appear to be empty. The shops have gone but the Imperial Arms, the public house on Old Road (top right), is still there. This picture was taken in around 1910.

The Ramblers' Rest, *c.* 1940. This has become a popular pub as road traffic has grown.

The staff at Chislehurst post office, *c.* 1900. The office then was a small house, known as Teatime, in Church Road.

Chislehurst from the railway, 1911. Christ Church can be seen at the rear. On the back of this postcard written to Miss Arabella Tring of 48 Richmond Road, Bayswater is the message 'Chase me round the chimney pots, Win'. Obviously Win was a bit of a wag!

Bickley Park Road with the railway bridge close to Chislehurst station, *c.* 1914. The trees lining the road have been replaced by houses.

Lamorna Villas decorated for the coronation of King Edward VII and Queen Alexandra 1902.

Crown House, Crown Lane, 1981. This building was once the original Crown Inn which was of considerable antiquity. It was badly damaged by a flying bomb in 1944 but was rebuilt in its present form using some of the old timbers.

Chislehurst village from the pond, 1906. On the back of the card is written, 'Dear Mother, Just a few lines to let you know that Junior will not be coming home until tomorrow, love from all Katie'. Local postal deliveries at that time were usually on the same day as the posting.

A postman's funeral, *c.* 1900. Note the small boy joining in.

The Governesses' Benevolent Institution in Manor Park Road, *c.* 1914. Built in 1871, it has been replaced by a less elegant building.

Bromley Lane near the crossroads, August Bank Holiday 1921. People would travel out to the Chislehurst area from Lewisham and Camberwell to enjoy a country ride and a picnic.

Another stretch of St Paul's Cray Common. The commons were enclosed in 1886 and 1888 by the Chislehurst and St Paul's Cray Commons Act. Before that time the lord of the manor, Viscount Sydney, excavated gravel from the land and created the ponds and dips that can still be seen. Had the commons not been enclosed, they would probably have been built on in this century.

The old Chatham and Dover Railway was finished as far as Bickley in 1858. The railway came to Chislehurst seven years later and Mr Wythes of Bickley Park constructed the Summer Hill Road with easier gradients than Old Road. Summer Hill Road cut through his estate close to the station; another highway where carriages could await the arrival of passengers joins Old Road and Summer Hill. In the Edwardian era the station approach in the evening was filled with a flock of horse-drawn carriages with footmen and coachmen in attendance. This picture shows the up line in around 1880. In 1900 the South Eastern and Chatham Railway began to double the tracks from London to Orpington. A second tunnel was built and Elmstead Woods station was constructed (1904).

The Old Cherry, tea and coffee restaurant *c*. 1930. Note the 'Cyclists Rest Teas' sign in the window: Chislehurst was a popular cyclists' destination.

The tearoom in the Sydney Arms in Perry Street, *c*. 1914. This was once known as the Swan.

The White Horse Inn in the nineteenth century. It has been renamed the Pennyfarthing. Why?

Belmont Parade around 1960. These shops serve postwar estates built across old farmland.

No. 48 Greenway decorated for the coronation of King George VI and Queen Elizabeth in 1937. It was the home of T. A. Bushell, a local historian.

The bombing of Farmland Walk and Greenway during the Second World War.

"An Institution is the lengthened shadow of one man."

—EMERSON.

IN these days of large Institutions it is very important to avoid impersonality.

MARTINS Bank has recognised this danger and has made a particular feature of its service to customers a friendly, personal approach to their problems. The branches of the bank are divided into districts, each under the control of a resident District General Manager with wide knowledge, and, with the care and consideration of your local branch manager, the "personal touch" is ensured.

MARTINS BANK

LIMITED

London District Office : 68, LOMBARD STREET, E.C.3
HEAD OFFICE : WATER STREET, LIVERPOOL, 2

Local Offices :

39, High Street, Sidcup ... ... Manager, Mr. C. C. RICHARDES
63, High Street, Chislehurst ... ... Manager, Mr. H. MONK
29, Mottingham Road, London, S.E.9 ... Manager, Mr. R. THOROGOOD

Mr Martin, the founder of this local bank, lived for a time in Camden Place. Martins Bank was taken over by Barclays in the 1960s. This advertisement dates from 1950.

Passing the Sydney Arms in Old Perry Street. On the back of the card is written '29 June 1908, Dear G. Arrived home safe after a good time. A bit tired, Ted'.

Webster's Pond was on the commons at the junction of Ashfield Lane and Kemnal Road, facing the house known as Woodlands. It was for a long time the residence of the Webster family. The pond is now filled in.

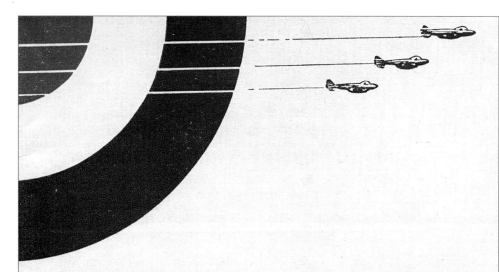

ROYAL AIR FORCES ASSOCIATION

(REGISTERED UNDER WAR CHARITIES ACT, 1940)

CHISLEHURST & SIDCUP BRANCH
No. 564

Presents

BATTLE of BRITAIN WEEK 1950

SEPTEMBER 9th—17th

PROGRAMME 6d.

TRADE FAIR
IN CONJUNCTION WITH
SIDCUP & DISTRICT
CHAMBER OF COMMERCE

Nº 2031

The Battle of Britain was remembered for many years after 1940. The Chislehurst and Sidcup branch of the Royal Air Forces Association was a joint group reflecting the combined urban district council and common community of the two villages.

CHAPTER THREE

SIDCUP

The hamlet of Sidcup grew up around the blacksmith's in Cross Road and the Black Horse public house. That part to the south of what became the High Street lay in East Chislehurst. To the north it lay in the ancient parish of Foots Cray. With the coming of the railway in 1865, Sidcup began to grow outwards from the area of the station: in 1851 the population was 390; by 1901 it had reached 5,829.

Foots Cray declined as Sidcup grew but it has always kept an industrial base through all the developments from water-driven mill to modern technology. Sidcup itself has remained residential, but according to the architectural historian Nikolaus Pevsner its classiness was diminished in the building boom between the two wars. Even now, however, the eighteenth-century flavour of mansions in their parks is not completely lost, although most of the large Sidcup houses have gone.

Lamorbey and Halfway Street were once in the parish of Bexley. Halfway Street has the oldest house in the borough dating from 1453. The housing development north of the railway line began in the 1930s but before then Blackfen and Halfway Street were full of hops, green vegetables and strawberry fields. Special trains used to take the strawberries to the London markets.

The Tomkins kept this florist's at 2 Craybrooke Road, Sidcup. They were still there when the 1931 Directory was published but after that the road was redeveloped.

The

Official

Guide

to

CHISLEHURST AND SIDCUP

Foots Cray

St. Paul's Cray

North Cray

Mottingham

Lamorbey

Blackfen

This official 1960 guide to the Chislehurst and Sidcup Urban District Council shows attractively the areas covered by the council, and the illustrations neatly bring together the two principal areas.

The Black Horse in the heyday of the horse and carriage, *c.* 1900. The Black Horse was first licensed in 1692. The 1861 census recorded an establishment of six live-in employees: barmaid, housemaid, cook, ostler, waiter and 'oddman'.

The Black Horse when the petrol driven bus has replaced the horse, *c.* 1925. The brewers Style & Winch, whose name appears at the top of the building, were based in Maidstone. Note the one heavily laden telegraph pole.

A picture of the High Street from the Black Horse, *c.* 1913. How empty the streets were then!

Dawson's the department store, *c.* 1913. The store had an overhead railway to carry money to the cashier by a pull on the rope. The building is now occupied by Somerfields.

Sidcup High Street looking west, *c.* 1914. Note how the roof line remains the same to this day. Only the shop fronts have changed.

The crossroads by the police station, *c.* 1930. The houses and gardens on the right have long given way to shops.

A postcard of Sidcup scenes, *c*. 1912.

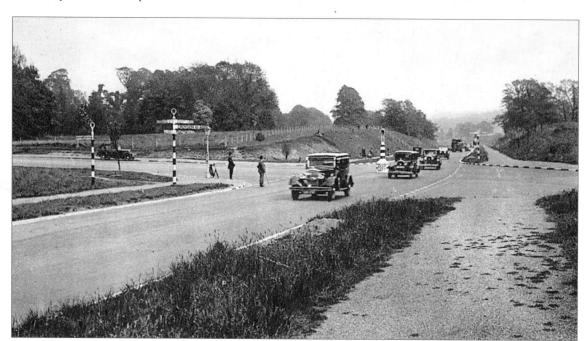

The crossroads to Chislehurst, *c*. 1933. The card is addressed to Mrs E. Pierce of Hythe End, Wraysbury, Bucks. It reads, 'Dear Mum and Dad, Thank you for lovely box. We shall write a long letter tomorrow. We are just going for a picnic. With love from all, Phyllis xxx'.

Frognal Avenue. This is the old road linking East Chislehurst with Foots Cray. It is also known as Watery Lane. Today it is often crowded with visitors' cars on their way to Queen Mary's Hospital.

The Avenue Tennis Club, *c.* 1914. This was situated at the rear of Church Avenue and was part of the Sidcup Recreation Club. It still exists and remains popular today.

The shelter in Sidcup Place, recently demolished. The postcard bears the date 23 October 1942 and was written to Mrs L. Clark of 7 Farrington Road, Gloucester, by Eveline, who was on her 'hols'.

The duck pond that used to be at the junction of Rectory Lane and Shelbourne Road, *c.* 1935.

Doug Holland's forge in Cross Road, 1930s. Old Forge Way takes it name from here. This business, together with the Black Horse, was the hub of Sidcup in the early nineteenth century.

The Green looking towards Freeby, *c.* 1912. Sidcup Place, to the right of the picture, was a school until 1933.

The Green looking towards Chislehurst Road, *c.* 1912. It is now part of a conservation area.

Boys posing for the photographer, Station Road, *c.* 1912. The former Girls' High School is on the left (now the Music Centre). Behind the fence on the right is the Congregational church (now Sidcup Community Church). Station Road was developed up the hill from the railway station in the second half of the nineteenth century. It comprised large houses for middle-class families who found Sidcup a favourable place to set up home within commuting distance of London. Nearly all the houses remain but are now mostly flats, doctors' surgeries or private schools.

Mrs Emma Hubbard, certified midwife and district nurse outside her home at 6 Church Road, Sidcup, *c.* 1908. She was a well-known figure. Born in 1864, she died in 1943.

Priestlands Park Road. This has changed little in the last 100 years and still has some of the biggest houses in Sidcup.

Lansdowne Road, a continuation of Alma Road. Some of the large houses remain. On the back of the postcard Jennie writes to Nellie in 1911 saying that she will be arriving in Warmington by carrier on the following day.

The Limes in Sidcup Hill. This eighteenth-century house belonged to the nursery on which the houses in Eynswood Drive were built in the late 1950s. The lime trees have been preserved alongside the footpath.

The bottom of Sidcup Hill, *c.* 1920. Foots Cray Baptist church can be seen through the trees on the left.

The former register office in Sidcup Hill which was demolished in 1991. It has been transferred to the Manor House on the Green.

The Old Ursula Lodges in Sidcup Hill. They were erected by Henry Berens of Sidcup Place in 1847 to be a home for six spinsters of the Church of England. The spinsters had to be over forty, have an income of less than £100 a year and be accompanied by a maid. They would be retired governesses and would be expected to teach in the two schoolrooms — one for boys and one for girls — incorporated into the building. The Lodges were pulled down in 1971, when this picture was taken, and new Lodges were built as sheltered accommodation. But six of the new flats continue to be supported by the Berens Trust though the original conditions have been largely waived.

Birkbeck Road, *c.* 1970. These cottages date from the early development of Sidcup from the direction of the railway in about 1880. Note the new tiled roofs.

A group of highly decorated houses at the bottom of Hatherley Road, 1970s. They are known affectionately as The Old Ladies, *c.* 1870.

29 Hatherley Road. This was one of the last of the large houses to be pulled down in 1972 to make way for box-like development. Hatherley Road in its Edwardian heyday was one of the more fashionable roads in Sidcup. Many of these houses were built by Mr G. Hawkins in the 1880s for letting or for sale. He obtained his bricks from Mr Harland whose brickfields were on London clay on the site of the demolished Longlands House north of Longlands Road. The last residents were Mr and Mrs Russell Gray who took this picture before they moved out.

The building of the new library in Hadlow Road on the site of the former Hadlow House which was built in about 1750. This photograph was taken in the 1980s.

Laudens in the High Street, 1980s. The shop has now closed and is vacant. The gate to the right led into the former slaughterhouse where animals were driven up Sidcup Hill from Foots Cray and beyond.

Leake and Hickmott's on the corner of Hatherley Road, *c.* 1980. It is now a charity shop. On the right, next to Mold & Russell, St Joseph's Convent can be seen. It has now been demolished and replaced by a nursing home.

Martin's the stonemason on Main Road, Sidcup, *c.* 1914. The house known as Adelaide House still stands in a builder's yard. This area was once a hamlet called Pound Place.

Longlands Parade. The postcard is dated 1906 and says, 'Dear J, I do not think you have got this one. I shall soon be starting now, have had until Thursday. Dad is getting on nicely. Fondest love from us all to you all, Yours lovingly, Eve'.

Marechal Niel Parade. This was built on the site of a big house named after one of Napoleon III's generals. The Marechal died before Napoleon was defeated by the Prussians at Sedan in 1870.

A fairly recent picture of some old architecture. When the original St John's church had its cloisters taken away they were sold to a local builder who incorporated them into the structure of this shop front. These shops were put up in Station Road in the 1880s.

No illustrated book on Sidcup should omit the towering Marlowe House by Balfour Beatty. It was topped out on 22 October 1966 by the Rt Hon. Pat Hornsby-Smith. It dominates the local skyline and is regarded by most as an unfortunate example of town planning. Butcher Curnow has now been replaced by a furniture shop. This view was taken in the 1980s.

Sidcup & District Free Press

Number 45.   GRATIS MONTHLY.   March, 1933.

Established 1820.

DYER, SON & CREASEY

W. F. DYER, F.S.I., F.A.I.   J. R. CREASEY, F.S.I.
R. D. CREASEY, P.A.S.I., A.A.I.

Chartered Surveyors, Estate Agents, Auctioneers and Valuers,

24, Budge Row, E.C. 4.

17, Montpelier Row, Blackheath,

111, STATION RD., SIDCUP,

(opposite Sidcup Station);

Telephone Nos.: Central 4221; Lee Green 0019 & 0975; Sidcup 223.

MONTHLY SALES at the LONDON AUCTION
MART and Locally by arrangement.
Rents collected and Estates entirely managed.
Surveys and Valuations for Probate, Mortgages,
Dilapidations and all purposes.

SELECTED LIST OF PROPERTIES UPON APPLICATION.

Our Sidcup Office is open on Saturdays until 5 p.m.

Nat. British Women's Total Abstinence Union
SIDCUP BRANCH.
STANHOPE ROOM, STANHOPE ROAD.

MEETINGS for WOMEN and GIRLS (over 14 years) are held on the
3rd Wednesday in each month at 8 p.m.
MEETINGS for CHILDREN (7 to 14 years) each Saturday at 3 p.m.
A WARM WELCOME AWAITS YOU

Sidcup Public Hall.
Evangelistic & Bible Ministry

Superintendent, Mr. G. Wilson Heath, Netherhall, The Drive.
Secretary, Mr. W. A. Harnett, Crayholme, Knoll Road.

SUNDAYS
11 a.m. Ministry of the Word.
3 p.m. Children's Hour.
6.45 p.m. Ministry of the Gospel.
MONDAYS 3 p.m. Women's Own.
THURSDAYS 8 p.m. Ministry of the Word,
with special Speakers.
SATURDAYS 8 p.m. Prayer Meeting.

A Hearty Welcome to all Meetings.

The Sidcup Recreation Club
Church Avenue, Sidcup

WILL WELCOME
NEW SIDCUPIANS

(Ladies and Gentlemen).

The Club is situated in the prettiest part of Sidcup, surrounded by beautiful country and offers many other attractions, comprising :

Two Hard Tennis Courts.
Three Grass Tennis Courts.
Bowling Green, six rinks.
Four Full-size Billiard Tables.
Card and other Rooms.
Fully Licensed Refreshment Lounge.

The Secretary will be pleased to send all particulars or by appointment will show prospective members round the grounds and spacious Club House.

CHARGES ARE LOW !

Phone 408.

F. R. WILLIAMS, Hon. Sec.,
57, High Street, Sidcup.

Mr. C. W. WILSON, A.R.C.O.

Organist & Choirmaster Sidcup Parish Church.
Conductor Sidcup Choral & Orchestral Society.
GIVES LESSONS IN
PIANOFORTE, VOICE PRODUCTION,
.   .   ORGAN and HARMONY.   .   .

Pupils prepared for Exams. of Associated Board
R.A.M. and R.C.M.

MODERN METHODS.   TERMS MODERATE.

Apply : 39, St. JOHN'S ROAD, SIDCUP.

Guaranteed Circulation of 5,500 Copies Monthly.

A page from a 1933 newspaper, a forerunner of the *News Shopper*. The estate agent and the Recreation Club are still with us.

Another Hatherley Road house. The writer of the card says, 'Dear Mademoiselle, I am at last sending you a view of our house. It is not as good as I should like it, for they have them so dark. I will bring another with me for fear this gets broken coming [sic]. Only two weeks tomorrow. We shall soon be with you.' It was addressed to Boulogne 1906.

The junction of Birkbeck Road and Clarence Road, 1980s. In this area lived the carpenters, the plumbers, the plasterers and the bricklayers who built Victorian Sidcup.

Walnut Tree Cottage at the foot of Sidcup Hill, 1974. Originally a small seventeenth-century farmhouse, it became a cottage for the coachman employed by Mr C.E. Shea who lived in The Elms. The Elms was demolished in the 1930s to make way for Sidcup Hill Gardens.

A 1950s steamroller puffs down Sidcup Hill past 1930s semis. Notice the Invicta sign of Kent on the front of the engine.

Another view of the old Ursula Lodges. Henry Berens and his brother, Richard, gave the name Ursula as the family crest incorporated a bear – *ursus* is the Latin for that animal. The lodges had a cloister and were reminiscent of the original St John's church which was built in the same decade largely with Berens money (Lord Bexley and Viscount Townshend were also major subscribers). The lodges were lived in until 1971 when this picture was taken. Only two ladies were there then and they were rehoused locally.

FOOTS CRAY

Foots Cray, unlike Chislehurst and Sidcup, was mentioned in the Domesday Book. The manor had been held by Godwin Foot in Saxon times (hence the name Foots Cray), but in 1086 it was held by William, son of Oger, who was almost certainly a Norman. As early as the eleventh century it had a mill which in the nineteenth century was to become a paper mill employing over 100 people, many of whom were Irish girls. Later the mill was developed as a factory producing radios for Mr E. G. Cole, hence Echo Radio. The extended site has been used to manufacture telecommunications ever since. The waters of the Cray have more recently accounted for the growth of the huge Cadbury–Schweppes plant. Foots Cray today is predominantly industrial but retains several ancient buildings and – here and there – an old world atmosphere.

Rectory Lane as it straightens out before making a fierce corner at All Saints' Church. This was the old main road to Maidstone before Sidcup Hill was built by the New Cross Turnpike Trust in 1781.

The so-called Tudor Cottage in the High Street before restoration, 1950s. In fact the property was once a four-bay, timber-framed, medieval hall house. A few yards further up is the Red Lion, built in 1823. It is said that the inventor Thomas Edison stayed there while visiting Sir John Pender in Foots Cray Place. Virtually all of the old cottages that were once in the High Street and behind have been swept away and replaced by two modern council estates.

Belgrave Place in Rectory Lane. These are listed Grade II and date from 1727. This picture was taken after the Second World War. The houses have since been restored.

A delightful picture of boys and men outside a shop that was part of Belgrave Place, *c.* 1900. The shop and the house to its left are no longer there.

The top two storeys of the Old House in Rectory Lane. This also is a Grade II listed building whose central part is of Tudor origin with early nineteenth-century extensions on either side. The frontage is very attractive when the wisteria is in bloom. The core of the ancient village must lie at the crossroads known locally to the busmen as the Barley Mow, after a pub that has been pulled down, or Catt's Corner after the owner of the general store who was a churchwarden at All Saints for many years. But these names will not last much longer as memories fade.

The bridge over the River Cray, 1980s. This was built in 1814 and widened in 1906 to accommodate buses.

The Seven Stars from the bridge, 1980s. The road at this point cannot be widened as the pub is a listed building.

One of the houses in Belgrave Place was a bakery. These ovens were found in the garden during renovation.

The High Street looking towards the bridge over the Cray, *c.* 1932. Notice the bull-nosed Morris by the Red Lion.

The Seven Stars from the side (now the entrance to Robert Greig's). The Seven Stars has records going back to 1753. In the early nineteenth century, before the railway, it was an important coaching inn. During excavations a plaster plaque of the Madonna's head with seven stars around it was dug up. It is now hanging in one of the bars.

The building of houses in the Grove, North Cray. North Cray Place was badly damaged by a bomb in 1944 and was finally demolished in 1962, the year this photograph was taken. On the site of the house and the gardens a number of well-designed houses were built, some of which have good views over the river at Five Arches. The spire of St James's can be seen through the trees. The lodge to the big house can be found at the corner of High Beeches with the initials of Robert Arnold Vansittart above the door. Vansittart was a descendant of Lord Bexley and a prominent landowner in the district. Many estate houses were built by him and marked with his initials. Sadly, today few remain.

CHAPTER FIVE

LAMORBEY

L amorbey is a pleasant residential area of Sidcup and was once in the parish of Bexley. It took its name from a family, the Lambienby-Goldwells, who established a house and estate in the fifteenth century. This house was rebuilt in the eighteenth century to become Lamorbey Park (*see* pp. 18–20). Halfway Street was once the entirety of the village, which remained a farming community until the 1930s when the farmland was sold to developers. There are several old houses along Halfway Street near to the station and the road names of the newer housing display the area's farming past: Old Farm Avenue, Old Farm Avenue East and Old Farm Avenue West. To the north Lamorbey merges into Blackfen at the Oval, a well-planned row of shops facing wide gardens and dating from the development of the 1930s. This has become a conservation area together with the Hollies estate and much of Halfway Street itself.

Station Road before the trees came down, c. 1910.

Burnt Oak Lane looking towards Halfway Street, early 1900s. The cottages on the left were built by the Malcolms for their estate workers in 1870 and are still there.

The first school in Halfway Street built by Mrs Malcolm. It is now a private property and is pictured here in the late 1970s.

Some of Hawkins houses built in the 1880s and later turned into shops north of the station. Since the photograph was taken in the late 1970s the shops have changed.

Oast houses for the drying of hops at Vinson's Farm, prior to demolition, *c.* 1930. The farm stretched all the way to New Eltham on both sides of the railway line. The road on the left is Hurst Road.

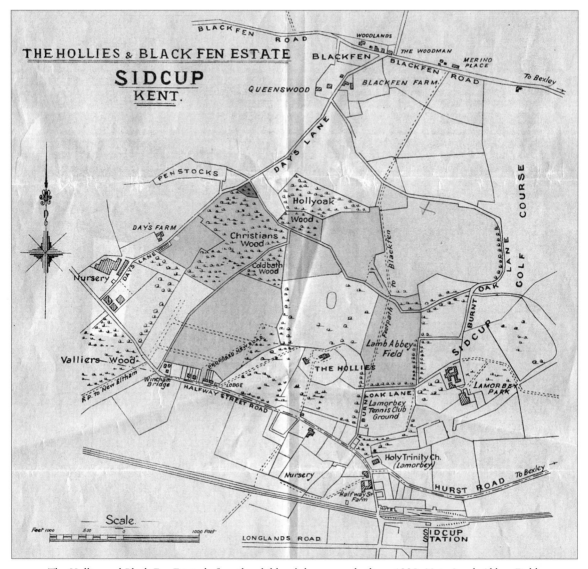

The Hollies and Black Fen Estate before the children's home was built, *c.* 1895. Note Lamb Abbey Field. There never was a Lamb Abbey. Can you trace the twisty Burnt Oak Lane to join up with Days Lane in Blackfen? The area was noted for its nurseries as well as its strawberries.

The rear of an old house in Halfway Street seen here in 1985 before reconstruction in the conservation area. This early Victorian house has now been rebuilt alongside some new homes of superior design.

The oldest property in Bexley Borough, it was built in about 1450, during the reign of Henry VI. It was a yeoman farmer's cruck house but is now made into two cottages. This and other old houses once formed the hamlet of Halfway Street or Lamorbey.

Lamorbey House in Halfway Street, *c*. 1914. It was demolished in 1930 and replaced by a Territorial Army drill hall. Colonel Beamish was a late Victorian resident.

The Drill Hall. This was transformed into a British Telecommunications depot and was recently demolished. A nursing home has been built on the site.

The Olde Black Horse before it was rebuilt in 1896. This is probably the oldest photograph in this book and dates from about 1870.

The Olde Black Horse in Halfway Street, *c.* 1933. The adjacent shop and cottages have gone.

The remains of the Red Cottage in Halfway Street, 1980s. For many years after the death of Miss Beamish, not long after the end of the Second World War, it fell into an increasingly ruinous condition. Good quality detached housing has now been built on the site.

Fern Cottage, 31 Halfway Street, built in about 1845 and pictured in the 1980s. This is one of several attractive cottages on the south side of Halfway Street, the nucleus of the old medieval hamlet.

Some of the Hollies buildings that did not survive. When the Children's Home was sold to developers in 1986 much was reserved for conservation.

Most of the large children's blocks were kept and converted into modern apartments.

Days Lane around 1900 looking towards Blackfen. This road took its name from Day's Farm. Mrs D. Stevens, writing about Days Lane at the end of the First World War, remembered Brigadier Martel and his wife, with their children's old Swiss nanny acting as cook. The Martels lived in a big house called Queenswood. Fields on either side of Burnt Oak Lane were acquired for the house and they stretched down to Days Lane on the left as far as a wood with a stream wandering on its outskirts. Mrs Stevens wandered the fields and woods, helped with the haymaking and corn stooking, picked mushrooms in the lower fields and crab apples in the woods for jelly.

CHAPTER SIX

BLACKFEN

Blackfen was first chronicled in the thirteenth century. It was a low-lying area, criss-crossed by streams. Two big farms – Blackfen's and Day's – dominated the area at the beginning of the twentieth century. The Woodman, a solitary pub on the crossroads linking Eltham/Bexley and Sidcup/Welling was first built in 1845. It was extensively rebuilt by Kenneth Dalgliesh in 1931. Many gypsies lived in Blackfen and it was an area that the middle classes living in Sidcup viewed with distaste. With the advent of New Ideal Homes Ltd in the 1930s, much land was drained and streams were placed in culverts. Cheap housing to buy was available to the skilled working classes who flocked to Blackfen and made it a boom town as the shadows of the Second World War approached.

Blackfen Road looking towards Eltham, c. 1933. Little has changed here except there has been a considerable increase in traffic.

Cottage in Queenswood Road that is
now a fine bungalow, *c.* 1929. A
caterpillar into a butterfly!

Clearing away the snow from the cottage,
c. 1929. To many of the early twentieth-
century inhabitants these pioneering days
without piped water or electricity made
them think of the Wild West.

The junction of Sherwood Park Avenue with Blackfen Road, *c.* 1960. The girls' school can be seen in the middle distance and the Chapel House peeps over the roof on the right.

The junction of Days Lane with Blackfen Road, *c.* 1936. The dairy is no longer there.

Smokey Joe, a familiar sight around Chislehurst and Sidcup between the wars and up to 1960. The police were often kind to him and took him in on cold nights. His surname was Curnow.

CHAPTER SEVEN

SOME CHISLEHURST SCHOOLS

Probably the first school was in the Poor House, where from 1834 to 1836 girls were taught to make their own uniforms of a green serge frock, a checked bibbed apron and a white mob cap. The St Nicholas' Church of England Schools were purpose built in 1869. As West Chislehurst grew so elementary schools were needed and Prickend National and the school for the Church of the Annunciation were opened in the early 1900s.

There were a number of private schools too: Farrington (combined today with Stratford House) was opened in 1910; Penthorpe School, which flourished between the wars, has now long been closed. It was quite common for private schools to start up and close within a few years before the 1944 Education Act as there was no compulsory inspection and school principals often ran their institutions as money-making concerns.

Annunciation School lined up for Empire Day, c. 1912. The headmistress was Miss Mudd.

Girls of Prickend National School dressed for Scottish dancing.

Annunciation Infants' School in 1914. Celebrating Empire Day became an important school occasion after the Boer War.

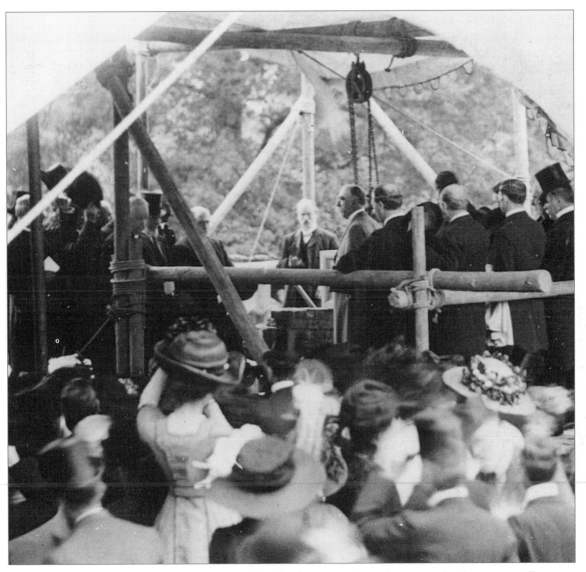

Laying the foundation stone of Farrington's School in 1910. Over the years it has become a well-established and successful school and additions have been made including a fine chapel, built of brick in the Romanesque style. All but the earliest buildings are by Crickmer and Foxley.

Penthorpe School, *c.* 1929.

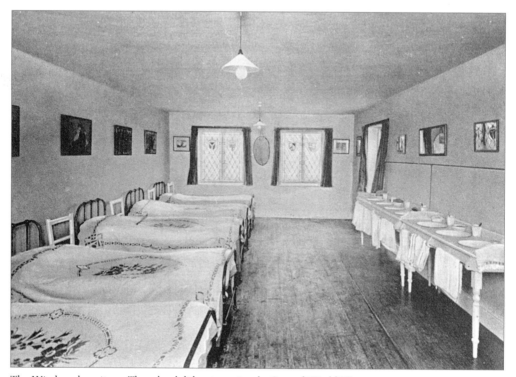

The Windsor dormitory. The school did not survive the Second World War.

CHAPTER EIGHT

THE IMPERIAL FAMILY
IN EXILE

Napoleon the Third went to war with Prussia in 1870 and was heavily defeated at the Battle of Sedan. The Empress Eugenie and their son, the Prince Imperial, fled to England and took up residence in Camden Place. Later Napoleon joined them. He was in poor health and died in 1873, being buried in St Mary's church. In 1879 the Prince was serving as an observer with the British forces fighting the Zulus; he was ambushed and slain. His grieving mother left Chislehurst and moved to Farnborough, Hampshire, where she erected a mausoleum to her dead ones and had a monastery built alongside so that prayers could be said for them. Chislehurst has many associations with the Imperial French family: Royal Parade, the memorial to the Prince, the former telephone code IMP, Eugenie Cottage in Crown Lane.

The inscription on Camden Place. It reads, 'Napoleon the Third, Emperor of France, lived in Camden Place from 1871 and died here in 1873. The Empress Eugenie lived here from 1870 and 1879. The Prince Imperial lived here from 1870 until 1879. He died heroically in South Africa in British uniform.'

The Prince Imperial, Napoleon the Third and Empress Eugenie in Camden Place, *c.* 1872. In her youth Eugenie was a great beauty. Half-Irish and half-Spanish, she came from minor aristocratic origins. She lived to be ninety-four, dying in 1920. One of her friends was Queen Victoria who made her stay in Chislehurst bearable when her son and husband were gone. Napoleon himself was rather a raffish figure who made the Paris of the Second Empire a centre for art, music and entertainment.

The Prince Imperial at eighteen. He aspired to be Napoleon IV, but was not prepared to seize power as his father had done. In the event his death at the hands of the Zulu warriors finished all hopes of the Bonapartists. His coming of age party at Camden Place brought huge crowds to Chislehurst.

The funeral of the Prince. He had attended the Military Academy at Woolwich and in spite of the fact that English was his second language, he came out near the top of the final examinations. Like his grandfather and father he was fascinated with gunnery.

The entrance of the funeral cortège into St Mary's church. After the funeral Eugenie insisted on travelling to Africa to see the spot where her son had died. On the way she called at another Napoleonic shrine, the island of St Helena where Napoleon I was exiled and died.

CHURCHES & CHURCHMEN

oth All Saints' church, Foots Cray and St James', North Cray were recorded in
the 1086 Domesday Book. The original Saxon buildings would have been made
of wood and with thatched roofs. St Nicholas', Chislehurst can be dated from at
least 1089 but because the area had no manor, there is no Domesday entry for it.

There were no new churches built between Domesday and the nineteenth century.
Foots Cray Baptist church came in 1836. St John the Evangelist church was built in East
Chislehurst in 1844. St Mary's Roman Catholic church came in 1854. Chislehurst
Methodist church was opened in 1870. Holy Trinity, Lamorbey, was built in 1879. The
Church of the Annunciation was consecrated in 1870. Christ Church opened in Lower
Camden in 1871. Sidcup Congregation church (now the Community church) was
opened in 1888, and Christ Church hosted its first congregation in Main Road, Sidcup
in 1901. St Lawrence's Roman Catholic church, also in Main Road, was consecrated in
1906. The most recent church is St Andrew's in Royal Park which is of a controversial
design and was built in 1964.

Canon F.H. Murray, Rector of St Nicholas,
1846–1902.

John Robert Townshend, 3rd Viscount Sydney
of Frognal, 1805–90. A strong evangelical
churchman.

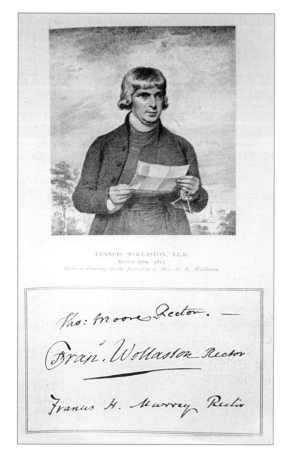

FRANCIS WOLLASTON, LL.B.
Rector 1769—1815
From a drawing in the possession of Mrs. G. B. Wollaston

Francis Wollaston, Rector of St Nicholas 1769–1815. He was the author of works on theology and on astronomy. He was a generous man who entertained all his parishioners – 2,000 in number – on the village green to celebrate the Treaty of Paris in 1814. His daughter has left us some fine watercolours of Chislehurst at that time.

St Nicholas' church after the disastrous blaze of 1857. The steeple caught fire and the bells and clock crashed to the floor. Within eighteen months all had been repaired.

St Nicholas' church at the turn of the
twentieth century. Canon Murray and his two
curates produced a series of hymn books that
culminated in Hymns Ancient and Modern.
The sale of this hymn book exceeded all
expectations and Canon Murray was able to
put some of the proceeds towards building the
chapel-at-ease at Prickend (no longer in use)
and the Church of the Annunciation.

The interior of Chislehurst parish church. There are many monuments celebrating the wealthy and
influential of the district. The Walsinghams, the Betensons, the Farringtons, the Sydneys are recalled in
flowery phrase.

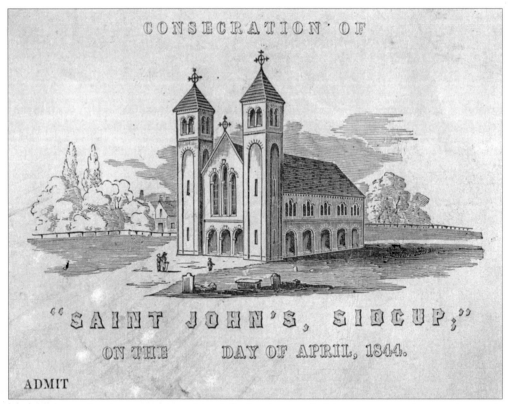

CONSECRATION OF

"SAINT JOHN'S, SIDCUP,"

ON THE   DAY OF APRIL, 1844.

ADMIT

An invitation card to the consecration of St John's church, East Chislehurst on 16 April 1844. The people of East Chislehurst had to go a long way to St Nicholas' church so they petitioned for their own. The materials for the new building were brick and flint. Mr Henry Hulse Berens the main benefactor wrote in his report, 'The contribution of friends enabled the fitting up of the interior in a far more complete state than he anticipated. The whole of the windows have been filled with ground plate glass presented by Mr Wollaston of Welling; an altar canopy of ancient carved oak by the rector of North Cray; a service of communion plate by Viscount Sydney; an altar piece on a pure block of Carrara marble by V. Bonammi depicting Leonardo Da Vinci's Last Supper.' Lord Bexley of Foots Cray Place undertook to build 'a commodious parsonage house', and invested a sum in funds for the endowment of the minister.

Today only the flint and brick pillars and wall of the original St John the Evangelist church remain. This picture was taken in around 1890.

In 1882 the Revd T.C. Lewis came to St John's. He added a chancel (the pitched roof to the right) and, because of the increased population, a curious extension to the nave (see also the previous page).

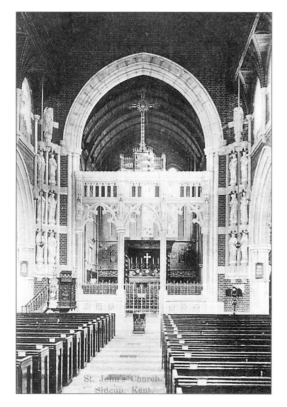

The interior of St John's. The church was rebuilt in 1900 to accommodate yet more worshippers. The architect was G. Fellowes-Prynne. The screen with statues of the twelve apostles was erected by Mrs Shirley-Woolmer in memory of her husband, the former vicar.

The squat tower of St John's as rebuilt in 1901. It was hoped to complete with a spire but the money ran out. In the foreground is a Grade II listed copper Celtic cross, a rare example.

The Revd Charles Pinhorn Farrar III, incumbent of St John's, *c.* 1870.. He had spent many years in India and translated the Bible into Marathi. His son, Frederick William who was to become Dean of Canterbury, wrote the book, *Eric, or Little by Little*. Rarely read now it was a highly moral story for Victorian youth. Frederick's grandson was Field Marshal Bernard Montgomery.

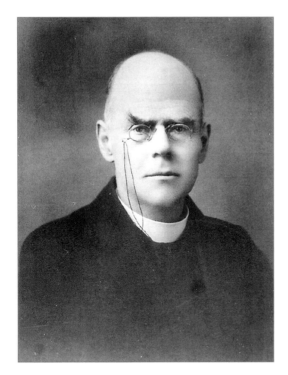

Canon Basil Spurgin who was vicar of St John's for thirty-six years from 1902 to 1938. He inherited the debt incurred by Shirley-Woolmer in building the big new church and suffered a nervous breakdown early in his incumbency.

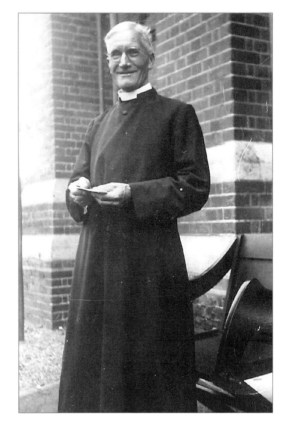

Canon C.E. Webb who followed Canon Spurgin, seen here soon after the end of the Second World War. He too remained in office for a considerable time – from 1938 to 1964. He saw the church through the Second World War when the great east window and Lady Chapel window were shattered by a V2 rocket that exploded on what was then Shepherd's garage (now the Toyota showrooms).

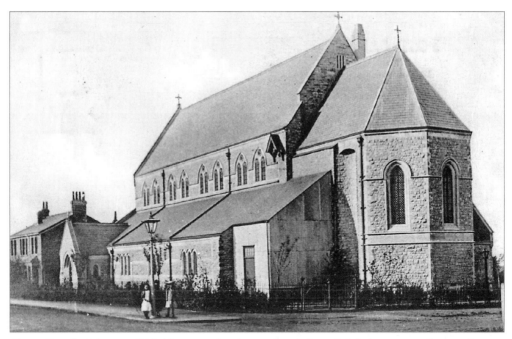

Christ Church, Sidcup *c.* 1910. This was a breakaway church from St John's as some of its worshippers objected to what they considered to be 'Romanization'. Christ Church congregation first met in a metal hut opposite to Queen Mary's Hospital before having its own parish carved out of St John's in 1901.

Sidcup Baptist church in Main Road which moved from its original site in Hatherley Road. This photograph was taken in the 1960s.

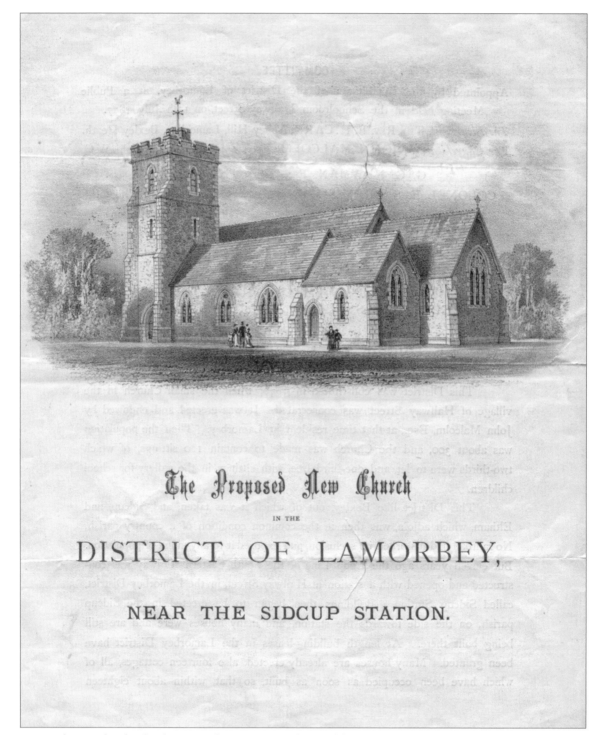

The Proposed New Church

IN THE

DISTRICT OF LAMORBEY,

NEAR THE SIDCUP STATION.

This was the plan for the new Holy Trinity, Lamorbey. It did not quite turn out like this: no tower was built. The Malcolms of Lamorbey Park though no longer living there were the main benefactors. Viscount Sydney was another supporter. Originally following Evangelical tradition, it has since become Anglo-Catholic.

Holy Trinity, Lamorbey, just before the First World War. It was designed by the architect Christian and built in 1879. After bomb damage in the Second World War there was further restoration.

The interior of Holy Trinity, c. 1914. It has the effect of appearing like a medieval church.

Sydney W. Groom of Holy Trinity, Lamorbey. A much-loved priest, he is seen here in around 1950 entering the church after its reparation following wartime damage.

All Saints', Foots Cray, *c.* 1900. Apart from the horse carriage, little has changed. The church was rebuilt sympathetically by Hakewell in 1863. The carriage probably belonged to the Rector.

Memorial to Sir John Pender and his family in All Saints' churchyard. Sir John lived in Foots Cray Place at the end of the last century. He was a pioneer of cable laying and telecommunication. This picture was taken in 1989 after restoration work which followed damage caused by the great storm of October 1987.

St John's Mission church, Susan Wood, Chislehurst, *c.* 1900. It was a chapel-of-ease for St Nicholas'. When Christ Church was built in Lubbock Road, the mission church closed. It has been used for commercial purposes including a soft drink factory.

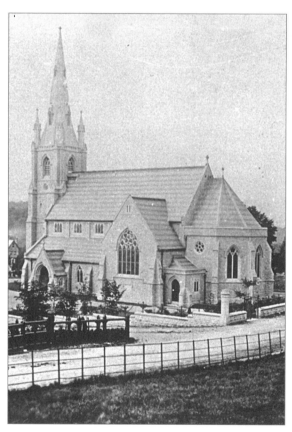

Christ Church, Chislehurst, *c.* 1890. It was built in 1872 by Habershon and Pile in the Evangelical tradition.

The interior of St Lawrence's, Sidcup, pictured between the two world wars. The church was built in stock brick by Edward Goldie (1906).

The tomb of the 3rd Viscount Sydney in St Nicholas' church. He was well-favoured by Queen Victoria whom he served as Lord-in-Waiting, Captain of the Yeoman of the Guard, Lord Chamberlain, Lord Steward and Lord Lieutenant of Kent. He died in 1890.

In the Vault in this Chancel lieth the body of
Sʳ. RICHARD BETENSON,
of Scadbery in this County Kᵀ. & Baronet he
Married Ann Eldeſt Daughter of Sʳ. William
Monyns of Walderſher in this County Kᵀ. &
Baronet, by whom he had Iſsue Eleuen Childrē
his Eldeſt Son Richard Married Albinia the
Daughter of Sʳ. Christopher Wray of Aſhby
in Lincolneſhire Kᵀ. by whom He had nine Chil-
=dren Richard his Eldeſt Son lies buried at ỹ
foot of this Tomb. Sʳ. Richard liued to ỹ Age of
78 Years & died ỹ 29ᵗʰ of Auguſt.1679.
Being then High Sheriffe of this County.

Wall memorial to Sir Richard Betensen in St Nicholas' church. Sir Richard bought Scadbury in 1655 when the 5th Sir Thomas Walsingham was arrested by the Parliamentarians as having supported the King. The granddaughter of Sir Richard, Albinia, married General William Selwyn, and their granddaughter, another Albinia, married the Hon. Thomas Townshend who thereby succeeded to Scadbury. He pulled down the medieval moat house in about 1730 and bought Frognal some years later.

ACKNOWLEDGEMENTS

I should like to thank Simon Finch of Bromley Libraries and Stewart Bligh of Bexley Libraries for their help. Roy Hopper was kind enough to check the accuracy of the introduction. I am grateful for the use of photographs, slides and ephemera from the following:

Bexley Civic Society 64; Bexley Libraries 7, 20, 21, 66–9, 117, 119, 122, 124, 204–6; Bromley Libraries 18, 123, 146–67, 196; Pat Bushell 19, 42, 77, 89, 105, 182–95; Father David Cossar 17, 59, 63, 76, 80–2, 118, 126; GLC Photo Unit 168; Russell Gray 207; Philip Lane 100, 198–203; James Mercer 29, 30, 32, 40, 58, 65, 70, 72, 83, 104, 107–9; Ian Mitchell 4, 12, 13, 24, 43–57, 85, 87; National Monuments Record 9, 23, 60, 102; Daphne Purdye 98, 128–39; Freda Skinner, 23; Christine Vines 62, 88, 99. The rest are my own gathered over many years.

The bibliography was primarily:

T. A. Bushell, *Imperial Chislehurst*, 1997.

D. McCall, *Patchwork of the History of Chislehurst*, 1963.

N. Pevsner, *West Kent and the Weald: Buildings of England*, 1976.

E. A. Webb et al., *History of Chislehurst*, 1899.

INDEX